Bent at the Spine
Nicole Markotić

BookThug / 2012

FIRST EDITION
copyright © Nicole Markotić, 2012
cover image: "Spine Book" © Sarah Mitchell, 2012. Used with permission.
Author photo by Don Denton.

The production of this book was made possible through the generous assistance of The Canada Council for The Arts and The Ontario Arts Council.

All rights reserved. No part of this publication may be reproduced or transmitted in any form or by any means, electronic or mechanical, including photocopying, recording, or any information storage or retrieval system, without permission in writing from the publisher.

Also issued as: ISBN 978-1-927040-34-8 (PDF)

PRINTED IN CANADA.

LIBRARY AND ARCHIVES CANADA
CATALOGUING IN PUBLICATION

Markotić, Nicole
   Bent at the spine / Nicole Markotić.

Poems.
ISBN 978-1-927040-08-9

   I. Title.

PS8576.A7435B45 2012   C811'.54   C2012-901063-4

Bent at the Spine

for Louis Cabri

Table of Contents

Big Vocabulary   9

Couples   19

Widows & Orphans   47

Bad Blood   91

Guests   113

BIG VOCABULARY

i

Indoor windows peek over haze, throw the role of doorway into fixed jeopardy, burst the remedial bubble. Shaganappi doesn't fizzle; Shaganappi doesn't

Link the vast grammar quirk

West of the coulees, the river jogs, the hoodoos idle, the poem immobilizes

Highways curve into psychoanalysis, heal the road, heed shoulders, divorce wild game, plant citizens

If, in deo, a cheese-grater replaces the blender, do you waffle the deco art?

I've been mongreling spouses for a long long time, ever chary, harried, choosey, cathedral-chique to chique. Interrogation repels ballistics

For twenty-seven sentences I plugged in remedial adjectives; I've pressed the Restart button 14 times; I own a pet numeral: ix

Humming through ashen teeth, the warden slipped his key through the catch, wove the yarn through parchment, snagged light through the part in his hair

The letter, sent

The verb, parsed

The poem, edited

Don't be such a worrywart, crave hurtin' songs, forget to mock *ii*

W8, don't 4get those 2 1-derful 10-ors

Floss regularly: qualified quellers stick between the front gaps

Toxemia cheers for a nicotine-patch, I applaud the tobacco patch – rowdy foliage for the throat

Figure out where to hang the washing, how many gardens grow gardenias and how many carrots – you get that yardstick, I'll haul away all planetary detritus – then calculate how giants handle economic excess

Get smart

Don't vex

Brown bears wander into leafy fiction for donuts and long-johns

Our bi-centennial ballads propose dried maples and Swiss long-division

iii

To aver, press two

Lullaby Orchids spew themselves over gravel, over asphalt, over nineteen nickels. Over the dandy cat

Benign orgasms hog two or more indents

Warts and all

Hand-in-hand, and-in-and (D_4&D_4 receptors for high school graduates)

Which colour is star-struck enough to v-v-vamp into purple?

Does boiling toothbrushes defraud the vocal cords? The gap-tooth? The operatic nickels?

Rogue cheats con swindles from a rattle… or placards from Eruditists

Bridal showers cascade out-of-order, sprinkle guests, spit on universal hours, submerge the one day

Make me a match, match me a flare, catch me a find, mislay the misaligned

Achoo!

Sheep pranksters hole up lambishly in erstwhile merry-go-rounds and pulverized trains

Shred the greens. Prefer salad forks to the King's spoon, diapers to folded blinds, biased absolution to skin's absolute caesarian

Come, and you subsequently pursue a faulty line of reasoning. Sever your employment, we refuse to let you mooch *seminal* egg yolks straight from the shell

Happenstance happens. Enjoy mints

Labia spells. Lip romance. Tongue the animation sentry. Try out:

Fluke of the grammatical infinitive

Plummet through columns until one semi-colon hooks your batting eyelash

Which colour implores: Oomph

iv

For instance, how vital is nostalgia to morning?

All's water that ends water. All wandering, fro and to, from and tom – Tomcat's culture preserves itchy

Add traffic violations

Don't expect alleyways in every poem, sometimes the artknot ties itself

In Berlin, a boy stole my camera full of hospital killing rooms. Homage to the image. One of my favourite shapes has always been the line – straight or otherwise. Enough for today's topic, turn to Appendix C for the back door summary. Time to unremember his dolce vita

The way the crumble cookies, the shuffle cards, the spill milks. That's bottom to my bare, hats off to exposed earlobes and implanted drums

The smooth table strokes back, arming legs and aching joints

I'm peeved, I'm gluttonous, I'm kneeling

Honey, want some loss with your hot sauce – mind the rhyme schemes

Inevitably, she swore a blue streak, leaving lilacs latched onto tomorrow's headache

Hagiography cannot forgive Tom Jones

Scratch rash decisions at night

That Berlin boy stole plastic souvenirs mimicking 10, 20, 50 Euros, but didn't make off with paper money. Sprinkle a few *stop-its* on his chest, and the photos will dissolve onto his skin. Wrapped like a mummy, bandage-swaddled, aching for a fidelity shelved in second-hand bookshops, he carried away one left-over chronicle:

Windows, carved tiny and culpable. In doors. In doctors' eyes. Only pretty as. Like I already told you: those hospitals preferred 20 x 20 x 20 coffins. Hades a welcome calm, a cool fissure of non. Word on this page. Never almost

COUPLES

succular

succumb to Winnipeg
suck on combs pegged to winter

snap crackle popsicle python
paste the cracks like clear snake facials

I disguise my wry face into no one knows
I'd die to be your guy – it's fine to know NO

dented rhyme misprints the chance
tends to hint at a margin miss

set me up for fall / drop / launch / crash
test the pump four times in autumn / droops / leaves / crush

flip the last page then duck
lift past the final peg due to age or elbow tucks

rearview mirrors look closer than a book jacket
cute ears press across kooky thumb tacks

kumbayahed past reasonable history or 60s tunes
come to jaded poet, reading his ability as tombed

or jack, posts by tucking fliers post midnight
then – sigh

seven slurpees for

underground poets stifle the awning
regroup to piffle in awe as he slings

with a frenzy you trifle with dessert
then rifle with nouns, just

slip in a double negative, purse
lips, nod to couple ablatives

gusto the tempo, open the gap
gussy up for tempura, pen gaping

tag this hailstone gem metallic
yep, got his stones genuine and tall

or not, that's an elephant!
rot, it's hats off, Eli plants his

trim autobiographies for a trap
I outta rim him, forget the strap!

wade through the fire alarm
why slim fires rough arms: *la*

my wander *lust* wanders
musty, just like standard wands

prevent emergency tours, and
the agency will pre-empt our vents

leftover wavepools twist flus into the birth canal
left-handed waving can feel twisted inside this cab

order now before xmas specials pout

she's a man in the hat, she's lost by a hair
she's a willow, he's a giantess, she's a bucket of air

sheets manage to parenthesize the hash air
see how he wallows, his parents ducts tear

the "hit & miss" prairies blend sort into like
his thesis praises the end of straw-smitten eyes

announcers emit the literal, with a capital W
we denounce the feral, spelled with a hiss

speak in tongues when you travel, it's how I get by
peek into a long ennui, reveal the ow in gatsby

it's an emergency, how we emerge

genuine mahogany weds genius megaphone
graphic webs gain too much

lights out or talk is cheap
try lying about the outcome or cheating with chalk

it's been a riot of insurgent peons
don't bend the rules for has-been poems

cry forward, sweep back!
causes are for the warden who sleeps with his back to the door

or are you attacking form today?
rare is the toady who forces your heart attack

when will you lay the length of your fingernail against skin?
He lies behind the magnet, his kin nailed to the fridge

open, a first edition provides fewer adjectives, more pronouns
she's noticed that heroes rarely wipe their feet at the back door

he tends to fist a rising pro-video fever
then, right, shepherds harken to the chèvre vibe

he's so ripe, he deposited foot odour at the bank
stripes deepen in colour when losing moot Babar

why whine about more than his cocky fantasy lore
why not love clitty fans-cum-tease-me more?

emergency nouns

ketchup and stop signs and neon electric man
can't say up and shouldn't trick No Man's Plaza

the limes they are my favourite
let me rhyme favour

a flight of
stares

expert Schmier players lose for the win
perverts schmoose more than in winter

fly by
straits

cantankerous she, leaves every eon
she can't anchor amour, shelves open eves

are you dieting by dusk? Do you waver? or fast?
Your yard flavour welcomes a rink-y-dink request
        huh-uh, that's my e-quest

langsam

lute terror brings pneumatic ringside autobiographies
lust tends to automatically jump-start inside 50s cars

far-awry and long aghast, treat me
to a far cry from ghosts and team songs

double sneezes rhyme with the echo onscreen
doubt me not or I'll tease your rhizomes, just so

walking can twist an arm or a neck
kings witness more armies than weeks

Fred's *ing* witlessly tweaks
fried wings with one fewer film to lengthen the eek

normal x stranger

leave it to sisters to be born in smog
lovely to see you both smitten in togas

yeast infections don't always harbour a gangster
get her an earlier fetching and I won't betray either

how come you come only once every half-note?
wow! you came after noting each nonce word

business tries – once a week – to ride busses
a bus trip replies – en route – to hide the kisses

work may be reptiles or outings or hickies
then icky worms in May repeat outdoor things, outdoor things

thugs haven't forgotten your birthday
but hug halfway to mirth, forego another trinket

white peaches in Paris
hats off to partial aches

rogue Achilles throws arrows at that hate-queen
go figure, the figure of Hades bequeaths mask insignia

my abode is a mirror, my walls impale knuckles
yada yada yea, this ode misses wailing
       an imp lunges west

nuke sandwiches at breakfast, ukuleles for tea
all Gordon asks is that you fasten your ribs

if you must break this pencil
trace your lips on my guest, on my trace, on my
      limp tongues

shake your blue thing

ezekial sprayed it, didn't say it
easy does it, buddy, we're trying to pray idly

reject seven toes and you'll half-way to Borderland City
order now, beat the rushes, survive drowning in rosaries

of all the pubs in all the hot-spots, he stumbled out of each
fall back into pubescence, tread softly, tumble with my honey

isn't taller supposed to not reach?
s'not talks, but to each her own nostril

verily they said, very, really, verrific!
rifle or mix it up, search, hurry, take charge – really

then every reel unwound clip by clip by
rounding out the dollar, rounding up the atheists

I'm still trying to nix the hurry, the beacon, the Argonauts…
Really!

slip Herakles under the cross and we'll witness tories
kiss me wetly and his lips will swell with wellness

I'm not done, thee shan't commence to broker a flange
do not mind when merchants break for love nor money

                                                      eggs or
                                                      honey?

the colour bleak

odourless sneakers spend pennies on the backstroke
don't listen to the lesson, sentry, bend the trend

how often does HD fit into a floppy disk?
show off the hidden talent of poppies and exits

egress, but
I digest

punting the elongations pummels the elevation
but clogs meet my feet like a tunnel, like aviation

prepare to greet your future granary
propose a toast, eat fine grains and chicory

I sing for the rhyme and for supper and for
this glottal stop

tupperware folds cilantro inside thyme
gotta run

bare-throated she rushed them one tooth at a time
are you through threatening the bushes with angina dentate?

an answer's as good as a rival
Anna-anna swerved into wood for revival

lucky bumper 19
burped by trucker LC

that's a wash
ants to ash

oh
no

trippingly she donated a sliver of kneecap to the horizons of zeal
don't pity the silver or kneel to reel her zoned-in capricious Ps

a block of bloke
locked the rogue, again

intimation imitation imagination magine

a nod's as wonky as a tight-lipped pucker
nobody woke up the tight-roper sucking on her key

it's bean a wile, sed the fox
teens, wild as Ed in his box

a borrowed cane sits gladly in the shade
row for tomorrow and canter lithely should it glare

a must begs for entrance, begs for media time, begs for begets
amens entrance eggs, mediate beginnings, forget to trace

a broken bounty brings plenty of *pain*
toking out lends bread to your kin

heading up seats beads on the rosary
knead here, eat wheat, pass the savory!

migrate in tatters, limit migraines to the skin
sink faster or skeletons form the scaffold

a hidden, a spoken, a folded, a fly
try olden, try coping, try knitting high
...er

race to the orphanage

elicit a retirement for unpaved aprons
lick where you tire, the amusement's prepaid

graffiti for centuries, green rhetoric for buses
retire when you're ready, great fairs to Tahiti

a slip on the sidewalk suggests leaves not pre-bagged
poems on the side, like boys we've left for punchlines

blisters on your nose couldn't come before winter
listen to the noose dangling four times per interval

or don't spy: the garbage excerpts go out on Tuesday
order now for the lunch special – each day except Wednes

fans of the genre hide an ace in the tuba
and that's where we agree, die once, only naked

take a shower for world trade

keep tracing the mark, continue acting the bard
step up to the dupe – oops, was that another cracker-jack?

a crease on your forehead is worth two bends and an awkward
creep into the foreground and bet weekends for double

above the neck provides hype against embroidery
below the ankles withholds telephone dogma

embrace the dry grains, leftover from October
metal clings when you regain a tuber-coated lover

every turtle pays double for velvet
hence the prayer towards sea level

after diodes, we couldn't turn the engine
double-trouble revolves their genes

water lifts and separates
two tables for ale

after pirates wander
into your former sail

tornado plays teeter-totter
revolvers tip-toe past offspring, bidding *adieu*

*a nomad, a man-made, a threshold, a
  spider ant*

take these, for example, take his, take 'em
place your stake in the copious rumours

in the lake
in the ex-fridge

you must have favoured a foreigner or three
why won't you anchor your bubble-gum for me?

a mess is as good as twice-taken
amen, said the balcony, falling from grace

bilingual hiding

ink moves warmly, then slips fast
mink arms lie slippery when they fast

a yoga minute passes lengthwise on the inhale
you gotta minute? innate ale lends gothic wisdom

she's got the smarts to hoist his leotards
a bard in lieu of lions, imparts moist arts

get
in

hockey settles outside; winter invents
double macho marches

vending machines offer the key to interior sides
make some doubt, set the lead out

why not treble today's Cézanne outright?
Hugenots blend the day with anne ou c'est, right?

are you worth the divided line? the pucker?
luckier in divination, are you worthy?

closed books brag more pages
bi-closet drag ages loose

a game's a foot in the door
poor flute thin as her name

every ampersand reroutes the detour
our very own amputee returned, turned

tag
none

schwa braves the wah-wah

ceiling fans whirrrrrrr, then wobble, then whwhwhwh–
what? *what?* we lie, hobble, cling. frantic to hum hymns

golf balls fly crooked when coughing
kangaroos unwind on the kempt hills

flog the yes, lob the rough rook, uninvite lithe kin
from their angular rants

C-sharp permeates the car and escapes through the exhaust
caped wonders meet rookies then sic after a spare hex

how many oceans hide from rain pellets? cling. frantic
sean wows the die-hard linguists. Fran raises her temple. clit

intergalactic breeding provides shady undergrad pedigrees
gallant videos define tin grades, sharp to the nth degree

a button or a tassel
sell the four abutments

wave to the west, shuffle to the south
huff and puff and wiffle those vows

a bobble or a taste
state "aaa" for Bob

I've seen witnesses watching the grand look
Lockness watches sell wit to five kooks

a bargain or a blaspheme
haemoglobin blasts gain bark

blond afros dread philosophy

he shouldn't have bent his blanquecino head to the platypus wind
play loads of wind instruments and you'll end this gusty typo

syntax travels the world, rhymes peek with bo peep
don't leave your travails behind: sin or tax? weep for old tymes

sake of the lamb, snake of the oil, beware the warden of sand
sake at night tastes best with dried soil, and rosemary, and raw nape

blank fros head into cinq times the ready lust
I'm heading for heady, I'm lost for your lanky q-tilt

Iym frosty
ahm piqued

pick an umbrage, don't skimp on the copious
brag or don't, um, skip pious pricks

segue or
guess

who thinks umbrage is a burp of a word?
thin takes propose umbrella as kinky howard

kandy from strangers
think candour, arrange cants

knit to the left, dosy-dosy

sod this, I ain't gathering nonsense, bud
tainted herds dub gringos, by tens, dose-a mud

her…

keep leaking the ménage into étoils
far stars trickle the ladiest kings

he married then married then married then wedded
deepen the parry, thrust, thrust

koalas hover over pirates
primates hoover aloevera

dust decides the foliage
ciphers the aloe lip, my liege

we wait
knit her dose…
        lose less

An Epilogue in Single

Who wouldn't cure canker sores and ear infections with a kiss on the bellybutton?

Split lips sink into cornucopia.

Wooden crosses slam into vampires begging for papal candyfloss.

Exploring springs from another colony messes up municipal back lanes.

Three years can be 20 percent of the rides you take on a bus or a bicycle.

Living in a hat leaves more room than a shoe and can help you finish a sentence faster.

Egyptian hieroglyphs learn to disguise the Loch Ness monster.

How about a cookie? how about green cauliflower before bed? how about Moses' snake staff?

Shopping usually takes longer on the coast, maybe the weather lied.

A meal on wheels can slip inside a smaller meal, another wheeled invention, a Headline.

Sasquatch used to roam across Ohio, until God invited them to the Rockies; now they tease petrified apples from avocado trees.

Jackson Pollock knew how to spill, just not how to lick.

WIDOWS & ORPHANS

"She's glad he wasn't old for very long."

grey schizophrenia dreams Canada. ancient globe technology and mapism. music globe-trots Europe. especially Montréal. leave the dual americanism and gender roles to listeners. stamped lyrics mediate the mutually 49TH parallel

local audiences suspect that ideology works

sue for Native land rights and an answering machine break-up will cover the evening Special

let that be a lesson: New Math eliminates the wrinkles in 2x2 flow. west grows old fast

trusting temporality implicates the wrist

try to end with a superannuated drum

"Men love porn & men love technology – yes it's perfect..."

to sex scientists : sleek metal reflects long lines of muscular blueprints

spiders worship mucus technique. everything possible in pop culture, except lunch. he leads lyrics to poetry blues pull. like the chronic *ing* in *rockchair*. ribald TV commentators don't know when to stop after the red light flickers stop

practice ghosts wave in the backyard

donor trifle can be critical or not. this depends on the blood level. leaving women out has always been part of the boomerang equation. new blooms close down the bulb. but open the window and you'll feel raw breeze. enter high heels as s handicap. perhaps a wooden stake or two. or throw in a cross. suckle the neck that feeds you. undulate four duet spines

such that working from *out* I would attempt to lose my voice my soft tissue as soon as I find it

try under the *a priori*

"I unbelieve times 2."

2 retired librarians don't know their mother tongue. except why the chapel they build might be a giraffe irreligious to the eyes of the beholder. randomly I miss you. uproot that raspberry bush to sucker behind the alley. yo-yos grow wild in the basement while the law rolls over its own bust enhancer. Repeat the trump card and flip the deal. laugh and you won't have time for the sing-along. go

other people know cunt and homesickness could be the same word. diction provides a cliché for how long it takes to reach the middle stanza of melodrama

and the winner is!

"Shift the pronoun and he loses history."

yet his gender remains intact. they congratulated Time for being older even though he didn't make the shift at any level of the alphabet. toothy print venues enabled him to scrutinize the 80s. so the age of writing represents hands-on gender. ruthlessly taken outside this metaphor mosquito coils recoil into spirals. stigmata in movies may trigger as many mysteries as madonna paintings

sure thing. gulp a cold and find yourself swallowing illiteracy in a church closet. the downstairs version. never heard an artefact comment on the smallest goal audience. even believing a general reader enlists poetry for Heart-of-Darkness porn

"No such thing as a prose poem."

mumbled the Cyclops. shining her black leather eye patch. hard plastic mimics cement. trial children leap the ladder. rig construction tumbles into the valley of faraway. yearly postcards line the ceiling. goes to show how many pairs of boots fit into one box. x-rated continues his morning breakfast to read that crocodiles have no tongue. except when he looks inside one there brags the rogue organ. not tied or mangled just limp and jaded and only slightly extinct

the font fades and 14 pages blew out the side window. well isn't that the way we harbour plot-line? each glottal stop opens the throat. treat me to a new typeface or send metre back to the morgue. each flyleaf remembers its copyright. true. each stammer confesses to grammar health

heroin could contradict this story or you could pretend these words belong to the same sentence twice. every time you save your breath, Hypothetical Barbara takes a bath

"How erratic index muddles the usual usuals."

surely after a night on the town I have more than trumpets on my mind. damp shoe laces and blood will not slumber. regionalism rarely points one-way. you know I'd love to *study* the classics but first there's the problem of wedding woman and her photographic gown in snow

we alphabatize cuz it's time for another decade of *Separate Tables*

stop or I'll loot the alibi

"Invalidate the invalid."

die more often than you jumping jack the grave. equal wit equals tone down the chanting monks and waiver twice a month. heroes know when to shoot their own winged horses. Spinoza thinks therefore we are. every supernatural wristwatch winds widdershins. shape the cookie cutter to match Xmas sales

see that magpie thieving from the alley? yield signs replace the stop when wedding rings fit around the entire hand

down for morning prayer; right up for afternoon squash

hearts lock. kill time between interrupted horseshoes and red toboggans. so if you believe in voting you believe Xs fit into boxes. subtract the sandwiches

slow down you smooch too fast

"There are some things a husband should never know ... whether or not his wife has visited the moon is one."

every neck bottles breath – his quiet hand – dares toward the throat remembering. gather brain cells and contact lens now. wait for his black leather bag dipped in the gutter

ripe oranges floating above a counter proceed towards the cauldron. nobody knows the troubles I've scene. endemic nicknames pose the deaf postcard as a phonograph

hide the crystal ball before this sentence ends. siestas predict local dialects. Spain promises naps

share each time you count to zero from the bottom. metaphysics donates rambling on and then and on

"No, only this country is universal."

lengthwise the basic question is a vernacular zero. originally my background was what I'd moved away from. mostly the long answers come right before question period. DNA explorations take a body farther north. how do feminist utopias subvert anyone else? every dot on the map

please sin

notice the family as stand-in for television. note the identity metaphors for green ketchup

plus four times four the cross lands in the airport while we grapple with slotted spoons and line endings. subtly leaving out her scalp rub. but I was going to explain about feminist utopias ... stories change

ensure the "make way for plot" plot. the road plan plan

new words harbour words. show shows

"She learned to speak English by folding the map."

pre-paid narratives begin with closure. eye doctors recommend most books on the shelf. faint tinge of red against the yay. yearn for glimpses of boys on the bus. slim down from listening. germ mothers and actual sentences block the armored car and police cyclist escort

tie up the books with used flypaper. rash across my belly. you may want me to waltz at your funeral but Hypothetical Barbara raises her pinky

yellow eyelids end movies dramatically. yucky chase scene and heroic underwater rescue. each stimulating phone call in time to intercept the homoerotic gazebo

oh blast the past. try again with a hand-painted jaw replica. accelerated sailing smooths the wrist gash

how butch is a motorcycle once the politicians hop on board?

"Doctors who inject the lethal sentence or supervise the execution lend the appearance of medical procedure to murder."

rate what happens if wine skins fill with white or red. die on a bus and your life sentence becomes someone else's grammar lesson

not even liquid soap keeps its shape. experiment with IF. fill with sand. don't laugh, he filled confetti to the brim. must depend on who's impressed

dire sentences sometimes end way before the period and sometimes well after. rubbing shoulders with that perfect dot can be a tricky landing

get the female body reversed as the verb of sex. x-rate my want to imitate stories that imitate poems. so why is it that during suicide week the rules won't thaw?

we put on a funeral for representational art. twice, eh? how easy to slip red slippers in the coffin. nostalgia throws a bent elbow into the grave

"End with an optimal illusion: othing but ooks."

scrabble dreams export their own punctuation. new clichés include stacks of booked worms. she's holding a bicycle helmet and reading its lip. please cross the room from the evens to the unevens. she'll justify that map. please edit in the dim light. tenses shift. texts don't dream for us all; last night I am assigned a seat at my own table but not before you are spoken your mind

divorced nicely. young silent letters, singing consonants – S, L, V – vows startle the academic. candy on your skin licks soft, true pinks. slip the L into other sentences. slow disintegration. not from glue but from belly puddle. elongate the vowel *hard*. *duende* can inflame lemon peels or dew. we watch and read and and watch and snatch. here's the body route: every left follows a right. tank down. not on that knee. envision stronger beating Rigid Eye Movement. test your sleep – plea bargain comes in at a bargain. nipples pierce. 'ello, orn't you going to call? lust singed. dimples bend. duo till dawn. nest inside the other knee. evident indent. tropical: let go

"On Tuesday Mister Crowfoot chooses the subway."

yahoo selected the Maritimes as the subject of biography. yesterday begins with a capital

letter to colonizing letter

rip lengthwise and twist. then pop. piling leaves to the left shifts the new narrative from political to by-pass arc. cuz she's obsessed with the linguistic other and writes a third novel later that day. you can tell the worst was her key-word list: takeoff – fireworks – subcontract – tailpipe – espistle. egg yolks rarely display manifest destiny on C-train windows

save the coyotes from mispronunciation and first graders

stiches don't always begin at the tongue. eyelets speak mouthfuls. select the cavity with the highest REM. meanwhile back at …

"Technically I'm psyched but I don't feel it."

tucked in disc. cuz visiting takes longer. Rochelle salt tempts them. must the house rent itself with those doors slamming notes? sand litters pockets. suburban wine can be so much more expensive

every time you slip my pen into your mouth your lip-print holds a bit of minutia

a propane tank slides down the river and a plastic factory explodes. stinging the air. repeat breathing toxic. conceal the late edition. nil times we've shared the same grimace but where? even her ponytail keeps getting caught in the typewriter keys. she purses her lips, she handbags her fingers. sure I continue to owe her letters but she never calls back

kidnap the giant vulva theories. sounds remarkable but what about the inverse?

even I have trouble with book-learning applied to werewolf law

whenever possible he encourages education to last

"Trudeau's ghost of a chance."

expose change to hosts who go wait in the car. right you're sure but I don't own his mountaintop

please be aware and be weighed. do not waste the throbbing tempo. only try tin. Not that I need remind you but : thousands upon thousands. sure we're sure

eight towels. same day same dollar. rank and file. evade the question

naked detour to the left. time to change the tune. each one over easy. you know the drill. less and less makes more and more. eat green and sleep blues. soldiers rhyme before bed. don't sass. speak of the devil. lights out at 0-60-hundred. don't ask. kites for sale and new flags in front of Parliament. time to sever the mutant limb. be wrong. gallop twice as often. never change. Eng gives up but Chang decides to linger

"Reverse Science Fiction."

no plot twists write inside a math problem. mere gloom crystallizes inside the computer screen. no sleep weeps in chorus. simply naming it Alzheimers leaves out your left earlobe. ethical bodies usurp red yellow pekoe. entirely in the medical sense

easy to tempt calculus backwards. sit straight and relax. x marks the spot. Tina asks James if he still favours print dresses. She hurts him more than her shirt. talk to Rousseau. up down and clockwise. expose the gum. mean it

twenty times two doesn't fool the computer. return to Go – over there – every man on board! Decide to remember one sentence from 1974 or three words from the day after tomorrow. wean him. moan or tilt or slip into the birth canal. last question

now if half a man eats half a pie in half a minute…

"Even we thought he was innocent."

treat bold facial ticks on he who takes winning for granted. demoted they say he's a hero. ovaries believe that for one year they stewed. drowning in cloverleaf

fondle the hand-held telephone. everntually there'll be more CNN than you can imagine. ephebe train with a boomerang from eastern Saskatchewan

nonce words fit oprep

please remember we paid for that genius. sectional looks the same from above or upside down

never engulf the gulf stream

my false fallopian clings to the church steps

sheer editing may prove too vital – lumps transcend the page – epidermis slips under. Retie your laces and you'll hop skip and a jump. pronounce with an accent for tissue reception. nouns practice all the time. eateries along the boulevard slip slide and song

gotcha

"Ab-original leaning."

go ahead and call me crazy but isn't Y3K the next wow?

words generate letters and letters inflate the comma and semi-colon. namby-pamby sign posts lean into the wind. don't jump from the aircraft. twice now you've gotten tired of reading words in order. right away assume the northwest isn't the best quadrant

twist stir and add. downtown meets ABBA. absolutely not said the rabbit to the hare. elevate your toes separately from your rings. slanted roofs reject neighbours. steady and slow. wizards have to conserve fingers for the wand to wave

expect more than a Time's Square countdown when your aunt's Down's Syndrome measures retro decades. slip in a discretional nod and feed the viewer her own hit series. speedy lips sink chocolate coated reruns. serve

"Eyes believe themselves ears believe other people."

engines impersonate viagra. attack the bark. kick-start cocoa beans far enuf. fortune cookies for the fortune seeker

round donuts but without the gravel. later the blind boy said he could see your $5 or $10 or $20 by stroking your face, eyes first

turn past the blind curve in the alley. you smell the mist but don't taste brownies or dusk. kittens wait for nerve endings behind their eyelids

she sees clouds but doesn't hear them

marinate the coffee in the shade. elongate his bone. enter the wow. whereif

"Feminism and a half."

foster care isn't the first time why she can't remember her lines. short breaks in the voice break the vice grip. put the emphasis on each book big in the 70s

she can't get used to the discount they've put on matriarchy. yielding such low low prices, see ten flags 2 short. timing and a guttural weep. pretend this is still a good time had by all

lately food isn't fashion

no way those adjectival qualifiers end with my you. until the part in Julia's hair makes me weep. put that way where's the squashed curve. every gesture with his left hand indicates speaker position

"Never bookend punctuation."

nevertheless her hand no longer blinds. she suggests fame has been caressed. duets mythologize caller ID. double lips full pout ahead

"Dictate the prose back home."

enclosed inside *prose* snuggles the French word for dare. enhance the inside poem *oh-um*. my lipsticked and labial teeth – how can he tell? lend a hand picking up hitchhikers and I'll earmark my passport lying on the highway. yearly long distance phone calls outdistance postcards. so according to Hemingway it's a candlelighted dinner. repressed phallic objects seem closer to a penis than they appear. reverse double eyes see double glazed. double chocolate. even banana boats float. the beach littered with expectant condoms and vanilla sundaes. so much for literary pros. so much for the prophetic beat-*ess* poet

"The capitalism of leitmotif."

formal elastics once snapped and hard buttons gone melty lose their skill. lazily refuse to substitute for one of the men on the board game

eventually the bridesmaid will reach for depot home. enter an already spoken for but still quite vacant stall. let in a splinter of biography. yes during the night after she cuts off her hands I watch new skeletons compose her garter belt

to gradually decide. each question mark should replace the period. dot

though high school wasn't the only place to fail a driving test. to be truly subversive one had to wait till 65 or over. repeat now

we were *all* escorting the escort: three cheers for dinosaurs on bikes!

sightseers witness the borrowed hypodermic

"Clinging to the fax."

Xmas will be here in minutes and they wait for returns. see the arms of the decade. eliminate the alternative in the centre of the word word

"*Do you prefer indoor or outdoor feminine hygiene?*"

expectant alabaster maiden assumes the edible subject position. nobody admits pleasure in chaotic sentence structure. entire keyboards have been labelled for less. she passed out instructions to an audience of poets: step-by-step; please be advised; destined for Tahiti; insert the A-tab into slot B. Berlin's secret was to listen to her lies. some graphic, cum bio

open wide for purple tin transformations of an otherwise ignored cankersore

etiquette of menstrual control demands personal choice at the supermarket. thinking has been known to lead to sentences complete or otherwise

egotistically if it happens to you it happened to me too. otherwise known as the *share* syndrome. effective group government and other forms of confusement. the way others mean narration. *now!*

woozy thinking has been known to lead to connect the dots, stencilled

drop two arms and one leg. gush like a fan in bad weather. right versus wrong fills the orphanage, eke out a thank-you. ugly tries on shoes. Swift chooses Team Chamomile as his hobby

ye old artefacts of the present tense but where's the body now?

"Which decades begin with two hits and a sigh?"

high-chair government's still pay-for-view. we depend on mad scientists and personal gain. notice how the ball rolls from normal to Igor. right when a skin of ice forms on top. panthers confuse grey with different shades of grey. yesterday's chilling thriller today's Jurassic Park video. oddballs share my adjectives. spear a shoulder to give them a ghost of a crushed amulet wrapped in deceptively soft cloth

"Half price! pre-purchase Pochahontes today."

your lover bent one elbow. wrung her hands and ran to the alley collecting pop cans and throwing away bottle caps. sometimes she makes bottle caps into earrings. sometimes yogurt. three times your best friend missed the tragic "if only"

yet every time he buys a BMW he stops making snide remarks about the rich

here lies the detritus she needlepoints into art. then he took out the trash. how did you wait for her? right after you knew he wasn't coming back. kites hit the roof when you fail at translation

never remove your eyes from your head. damned if you do. open up. put your cane next to the umbrella stand. downstairs is too steep. please watch your step. press firmly

"Yes and nO."

open the door
                open the window
                                open the underclothing

go east. touch the rosary slowly and with fire. each bead leads to the next. time to pull the plug. going up?

plus equals seven. nine times out of ten. no stopping. going right down to the toes

sort through those railroads and *unpack* the landscape. ellipses proliferate. expensive but bulk prices demand Freudian units of composition. now that you know us do you want to impose one pattern or recognize two? only extra credit when you hand in your work with colour. respect the border; respect the red line on a green page. evidence can head both ways – south or east? tear a page from the atlas and watch the abandoned spine shudder

reverse the sentence – end with a capital. leave well enough lonely and throbbing

"Gesundheit."

then she twists her wrist around until her arm faces ahoy. you know how it goes when the alarm clock rings too early. yesterday wasn't finished. do-gooders arrive at my door-step in twos – sometimes they invite me in. no sense waiting for Miss Manners. somebody had to hope somewhere. endings await. the comma crawls towards an invisible cave. except Plato had already joined the chorus tiny bubbles floating from the corner of his mouth

"healthood" wishes

single words climb an artificial wall constructed despite gravity. yolked up against the brittle shell, leaves press inside library books, socks unroll on the floor

remember when we splashed inside the fluoridated catalyst? t'was all for the want of a teeth clamp

people recuperate astrology as higher ground for the bildungsroman. now serial *this* hubbub, but stop in time

"... et tu big brute?"

earwax isn't the best way to recycle newspaper. remember the primary colours match the primary directive: evolve then squash

he really does absolutely certainly believe in truth. Hathaway and Gumbo. order now before the lights go out

testy confusion about who's a vampire and who's driven all the way from Bellingham in a van

no need to panic, cuz I'm paying a professional mother to worry

yearning for equators equates Colette's collateral age

E-S-S isn't how you spell "s." sluts put their periods inside the q-mark. kinky doesn't cut it here. "e" hasn't got a proper spelling

go sue the government when you run out of invisible ink. kerchief gusts from the north. he's British that's why

yesterday's day; Yugoslavia's minute. elephant beards grow against the grain

"Nine minutes of non-stop news."

shyly the perfect villain presents his sideshow – weary acrobats and overfed comedy. your letter demands too many details I have set it aside. emery boards and hollow lipstick tubes and foundation rejections

Sincerely evokes your name

empty? yes more than no

overlook the hints not the handcuffs and spiderweb clues. suggest a flexible tightrope not telephone tag. got to measure Dorian Gray. you give more than a portrait less than the local coinage. evidently he kept at it till the ropes uncoiled. direct idol. listen to me preach how the same year she died her son became famous for his neo-romantic vultures. same with his tilt at the windmills his whirligig tulips and his random fauna

"All journalism is auto-journalism."

moebius strip – purple shaded newsprint – tinted edge fades towards lavender. rather than make a point I digress towards giraffes in the bathroom. more room for necks and another chest. travel towards an opium looking glass. 's'no matter here's the wit of the story. yellow or cobalt blue sneakers beyond the orchid. dappled colonels signal aim and named borders. spoiled mirrors become the main currency of online diaries

share each other

regulations slip past the licorice towards an open x-plane. every tiger regrets orange. every photo prints the headline

end of story

yep

"Pants on fire."

evenings frozen fanta offers the end to moving day. you should lift from the knees. soon followed by cold appetizers and another film about Jesus

say it: this time the cross won't shape-shift into costume jewellery. your blood leaks from the inside out; try burning sugar when it's already in the candy. you must know how to fake laughter to make the slap convincing. go easy on the tattoes, she's flaming tonight. they wanted so much more than a winnebago in the grand canyon. nobody paid for giant pandas and this rusty rollercoaster

rhyme the lilt of your tongue pronouncing the labial L

like catholicism isn't nasty enough for you

uterus; syphilis; stem cell; liver spots

so you'll always wait for the transliteration eh? history repeats peppermint gum. me first, them last

touché – éclope. end of prescription vow

"Women in veils epitomize the sexy; yet men in veils – simply ridiculous!"

shifting stereotypes pack for the honeymoon. neutral sexuality dresses the body exhausted by uniforms, shoved by the Beggar's Opera into a moral universe. except we read the state of the individual studying the state of the body in 1711

11 men invent the possibility that women do not require an orgasm to achieve pregnancy. yeast infections either

Rapunzel property melts when rain hits the cardboard brunch specialed: dog-eat-dog: grapes peeled inside-out. this morning and by someone else's scruff

"Five legally-blind curves."

somebody release the thready remnants of punctuation gone wild. does air escape from raisins or exclamation marks from bubble wrap? precisely, yellow clocks tick closer to noon than midnight. they speak their lines then hold the caesura

all sentences promise dialogue but who will etcetera the margins? *so what* asks Fred Was – *so what?* – telltale poems can act perky in the morning, grow operatic at dusk

kid, do not ask for directions or ignore the help desk at the bottom of the escalators. sleep in. not one of them recognizes a 2ND helping as editing. go lightly and step right up. play dumb. be right back

kin knows skin

"Nowadays Jesus always longs to be in the midst of the tragic."

Colette's whistle covers my harelip my pink-eye my spina bifida. afterwards, she describes how her three husbands rotate 9 x out of ten. notably while he was convalescing they printed new maps. so far the grave has quadrupled. don't bet on siblings related by porous cracks and damp earth. how could he be born in an invented country when he lived to recognize the narrator?

right after addressing the letter I phoned my mother to pick it up. put that way why not show the transparency before spoiling the beans?

she normally won't wait for hypodermic translations

"*Stir and then add.*"

dumb faith falls on tasteless ears. should immunity be related to handedness? some levelling at birth enhances my eyelid itch:

> : hand-over-hand
> : hand-to-foot
> : hand-made
> : hand it over

rivers don't run. neon signals highlight punctured condoms. stand on pins and needles sad rooms show off Caliban's horse and buggy. your habits form decades before the rule book. kleptomania exaggerates, skimming the fables. staring is the only time I've seen you seeing. going anti-clockwise loosens the bank rate

ever wonder how thieves break-and-enter during a waltz? zoom in, nobody will turn a colour-blind-eye now. wait don't run. nobility duplicates goth. Herakles is the emperor-lover who bides his time when movin' on up. pester the climax of a long haul

lastly, you end with a bang

go the distance. expect

tariffs

"Star Wars available for 1899."

9 x out of 10 the body metaphor removes his liberal hansom. move over buddy, you've got a riot to curb

by following the red line of the debate she accidentally recognized the narrator's teeth. his not the only way to tell stories. sub-plots provide a structural amnesty and necessary apple peels

say what you want about identity, you still won't choose door number two

"Oh, hey, you don't spoil the fun."

nightly he sang the off-whites

sugar sugar twist and shout. this isn't the only place the word word repeats. side with the frontier and trifle with the whole class. slip in a line-break when the reader's not trying

"Gone fission."

nuclear agitation shivers the micro. opposites overact.
tell them my favourite eggs come from reptiles

swoop to renew

BAD BLOOD

Staying In

a boat skims the surface, plastic rudder aligns with the pond's sundial, the canons prepped and aiming. toys for US

who let the cat *into* the bag?

curtains drain the sun, your air conditioning follows Mars. I'll bet it's noon, now. I'll bet it's break-time in Copenhagen

worry from your lower back, down. a crisis of German emerges from the ankles up

do you fing-er, or do you fing-Ger? long-er, or long-Ger?

aqua naps help cut the string that pulls maps closed

but only by name tag

there's been a pneumatic leakage, a quarantined seepage, lay people lay about, their intention is freakage

my angle, usually indigenous, remains bent at the elbow

thigh high, my big toe plays abacus in the cricket park, a bat per person

we're all thumbs today, meaning my finGers are toe-like

close every ocular door with a deaf testimonial, and remind
the lip-reading alligators that kennels proliferate

ken you ken where I'm kent?

hurry and ketchup, the sundial's ticking

wrinkling the cut-offs

Not only Echinacea Purple Cone, but dried Arugula and Potato Vines. A berry crawls across the rough cement, thirty-seven moths sneeze irregularly, and succulents refuse to believe in westward shade.

Calandis blows on her Peruvian flute, covering the middle tubes with her mouth, and Shao-Chiu wears his spider-man mask. It's too big, so his nose hole sits on his forehead between the insect-blue eyes. Shao-Tien climbed the windows, Zorien lurched from the television. Pleats in their shirts mean ironing might be closer than you think. A popsicle during the heat wave simply

Motor vehicles insist that twelve times twelve equals, but does today count if it's past midnight?

I meant to look up IESB, but Firefly parodies took over.

A racket of scrambling, a drip of Shala-sweat, a wrist-bone releases, and fingernails flutter to the tiles. I have counted up the list 49-million times and the answer always equals.

Sonnets breathe 14 yoga inhales. Each one a pause, *pause* in German. Rush home while the rushing's good. Ghosts slip up as often in the mortal world. Could you walk that way? Do you bury saws? Two screws in the lawnmower, one above the kitchen counter. Check. Don't dismiss this information as poetry.

I'm still stopping.

The mask off, but the mitts on:

Gelati and Canadian Tire, or miss hedge, or three bets past

    a cone and one cup.

Holidays for mid-week. Who says being a wimp doesn't pay?

                                        Fleck it, or feck-it

          former dairy plays fort

a fleck of the feelick, a dice of the trice. Whyn't you treble, whyn't you play nice?

Don't stop for the soy-train, the gravy keeps comin'

              why-n-dot: street names for tunes.

I've explained and explained, but dying won't hunger

      just like   gifting for beginners.

Trade union station offers mini-donuts and Rah-rah-Rasputin raspberries

                who know what text's next

                              the hunted more than the Huns

won't sneeze for the pope?

Pass the mike, pass the class, pass the tenth of the twelve

    matching shoelaces
    stringing an instrument apart

                                        why-n-ot?

at risk or at least?

sloping from the TransCanada:

> a road crew to repair the prairie rain that slid
> the hill down the sidewalk

> three riders on one wheelchair, chasing cross-traffic

> a pedestrian bridge where kids leap up, just as
> the cars pass beneath

> used spiderman webs, dangling from rescue trees

> wading pool asthma

> and three blackbirds, pecking at peanut shells
> beside the hot yoga shala

could tomorrow pack in murderball and taxes, a porch sonata and processed wedding speeches, emails to two Karls, and leg passports?

when *didn't* hot-and-bothered last all night?

but how much ink on paper defines a *thorough* edit?

A Voice, then a Crow.

friends fly east, west, and north. I sit facing south, in the shade, late in the evening, on a flat piece of cement, dying for loopholes

and when tomorrow isn't what the early-bird brings?

Adjectives and Adverbs

Seven Monks with European accents kneel blessedly on the even stone, weep regularly beside the last corner, sigh

Protect the vital months, pause gayly at the beginning of the second page, wait for a new pronoun in the mirror-tricked corridor

Include the bent people who only bend their knees one at a time, rule the bee multitudes who lap at honeycombs, who lap buzzingly at combed honey

A buzzing indicates comas that are beginning, or ending
No way to reach the body in time

Adversaries and Objectives

Seventeen souls march away from the hell-mouth, the hell-tongue, hell's retainer, march blithely, march determinedly, march madness   soul or spirit?   sprite or sprang?

Protein is vital, be sure to remember more than languidly, more than umpteen times, more swiftly than a border mammoth

Inches from the edge, I reward you gorgeously, colossally, gargantuously

A B C – weighty matters matter. Call at the final end or the momentous finalé; nobody reaches the end without great undo suffering; paying one's dues, finally, on time, surprisinglyly

bad blood

at the peak of a pin-prick

      how slow a devil's dance, how honey-dipped mauve?

tomorrow rests within the grammar of a flip-page of Sunday hierarchy

        when to approach the frayed cable, the prosthetic cheat, the live wire?

after all hours, when there ain't no

      resist resisting or require a fast-forward zoom?

      resist resisting or require a fast-forward zoom-in,
                                    zoom-out

forget the teller. forget

the drip-drip-congeal of   *his-her-them-mine*
that ends   the end of the arterial loop

                                ain't now

at the what of idiom

heretofore, the operative of grandmothers and Kino bikers

she didn't slurp her pronouns, just gobbled the walnuts and fireflies

"at ease" slips into "at east" – where we lean, where we croon, where we chastise

        a thousand sections overlap with 14 words.
        and then he dropped the period

saying is believing is pretending is bargaining. that inging belongs with buzzing longs

a day or a month, travel to make use of the calendar divide; dive idio, live slides, sliver of lent, levers that idle until you

I keep reading "what" when there isn't a "when" – who leans?
   who croons? who chases? soldier caps capture as fantasy
   blends caress. stroke. petting. re-award
I keep reading soldier on, rapture is antsy. bend and rest.
   stoke up, tip forward

easy to slip into west and north. who binds the binary? who lifts the lips?

water warming by the hearth. or dearth. order on earth plays
to the same tune as man-crazy global. a glo?al stop
[stops]

sons and nets

yes, word-play still persists, yes yet

formica as dedication or devolved votes or keener

hasn't there been enough rain in Vancouver to outlast the
decade? the decadents want more

      bookworms, slithering towards unstitched hems

whyn't you call? over the moon, over the clover, over-easy.
just: over

a special or a spec
tackles the underline
wrestles the xmas wreath

      who isn't mourning a coffin-sized newspaper?
      last one home is an empty nest
      messy, but effective   nosy, and primal
      a word isn't sums isn't smut isn't mutter

yes

it is what you say, what you pray, what you breach inside the
work canal
and ending sl

because the brill ants
plod on   up hill
down slopes the fair
dow nope the flairs

yep

thermometer quivers

there isn't time for twenty double-takes
nor the time to reread the funnies

wanting having doing trimming
        a nose or a placebo

dragon-chest hourglass? (pistachio image for pirates, level child's coffins)

filter the watercooler
                gossip eats fangul
a chimp glues see-through snails to the gutter
don't deke out a deker, 7-decker, cross-pecker
stripes wrap his torso in spring fashion

        a mess of a mile
        a smile of a kilometre

ribbons bonus orangutans
the stop bites against enamel laugh lines
I am forever holding up
high: above us, below we
I amn't ever riding through
a you or a them
now

Oval Maps

Dear Embellished Mood:

that's what Nichol would call them, or so you claim. because the adventure is in imperial measure – too *back-in-the-day* for linguists to decode

why not wine in sunshine? tubs in spring? burnt stubble in the explosion of winter?

protracted hair, sticky-out ears, swimming every day, smoke-rings you return at the altar, and squished lungs in Cuba, and one last

How much?
    49 million gallons.

How long?
    49 million miles.

How soon?
    a gazillion pebble minutes, a baker's dozen of a year, a phonetically-spelled Era

Erratum. Erratus. Error. and each byway, triway, lengthways.   Froth

GUESTS

George Bowering in Joyville

try sailing through the mud when the wind's full of advice. a
    metaphor, or a margin – who skips best to the strains
    of a violin?

rain escapes Vancouver but it's desert here. Badlands. crop
    thirsty. ritual hail. try Kamloops in the morning then
    Boom-Boom at night. we talk. you joke, quote Freud
    and Jung upside-down

here is the point: letters import form. listening to you write,
    I hear regular blue and I hear chaos blue. pronouns
    pronounce intercourse to each other, change their
    minds, collapse onto mirrors and grids

names & addresses keep a record. the foot of Mount Simile;
    the head of the beer stein. 17 people play baseball
    in the essay. forget the word base. you leave initials
    spattered everywhere. not clues so much as people,
    touching

the next story begins with sticks and ends with a pound. your
    black-and-white hints at rattlesnakes but types 27. a
    scrawl or an eight-track. don't wave

heroes in the womb embrace trumpets. cackle sports. hug
    the seventy-second person. unbreak the salt-shaker,
    unsmoke the bamboo

but here I am, trying to play the saxophone. trying – again
 – to hear from the shore, drunk defiant, chanting. you
were kicking the sea furiously. the poet among us

don't sink

January 9: Before Kroetsch's visit to my meteorology class

thank you for boosting precipitation in Alberta. I confess I have always endeavoured to write the weather into line-breaks, wind speeds as enjambment, cirrus as infernal semi-colon, today's high as the exact moment I read *The Snowbird Poems* aloud and hear you perusing Jack Spicer. The space between breaks a mutual breathing.

You begin me beginning. The Chinook stretches and reaches and pulls my exhalation across the prairies. Louis and I passed beneath Manitoba last week, when we took a cross-country detour to visit Lorine Niedecker's birthplace and home town. We started in Windsor, drove to Chicago, then through Wisconsin, up towards Saskatchewan, into Moose Jaw, and on to Alberta. At the wheel, I quoted from *Alberta,* citing driving records and crocus alerts and overly coddled spring gardens. I craved myself back into the prairies, your prairies, back into provinces where Schmier and the rules that don't make logical sense, make sense.

You remind me, when you repeat "diadem" back to me, that ancient Greek does not accommodate the word blue. How to crown the poem without a pure lambent sky? Lorine Faith Niedecker lived in a small hut by the Rock River, her mother's breath supplying the room's temperature, and wrote, "don't be afraid / to pour wine over cabbage." She is buried in the same grave as her parents, her husband's headstone a footnote beside them. On the family stone, "Neidecker" posthumously insists on e-before-I: direction is important in weathered stones.

What is it about the grave, you ask, that institutes plot? I can only answer with Picasso blues and wavering humidity, with the idea of horizon flames on a crown of winter, and with snowflakes sprinkling over your head in the dead heat of a Calgary January. You lose yourself in disproportionate narrative, on purpose. And we smectite readers follow, determined to unbury the plot, unspell surnames, unpave the TransCanada, and unwrite the inclement page.

In between morning rain and afternoon hail, you noticed what I forget: pronunciation matters. And the invention of the telephone *did* change how we write.

Sunday Morning, Making a Break, a Sharon Thesen September

I share your "daily effort to solve / the puzzled heart"
that perforated muscle
contracting and
                    erupted

from a 747
mumbling without another word

holds its mouth in my palm, its dry lips a seamless another
purr

a knot rehearsal

        in ugly theatre fatigue
            –ghost tempers, basement fuse, hand blooms

"(branches for arms, bark for skin) / tap a little more love"
speak the one-eyed, one-tongued
into
the cringed body
        I, too, leave and
        don't believe
        that long distance
music leans

and you – unaspirated glide – yearn and pronounce

my quick pulse
        to the quick

quake pure and swollen and artful
        an awful pang in the belly, a Kamloops bruise
        my mouth become a longer dash

Susan Holbrook's hymn portage

do you dally in the outback or back out yodelling? I've heard kangaroos cough and possums chastise and a museum gopher cry, "help me. pleeeease, help." if eucalyptus trees shed bark, then shouldn't Joey fall tail first? why don't watches run widdershins? why does the beach slip seaweed under its lip? why don't you press more numbers than you dial? done. sarcasm and lilting chore-rhymes, movies made from loyalty and beer-flavoured chips, who wouldn't choose upside-down as a style or typo? meanwhile, you visit droughts from the mirage down. root for the carrots, they see well enough into curved arrows. what else traps the ocean and the jungle? repeats the boomerang and the koala? meets my mate and her helpmeet? a lonely extra or a satisfied custom? an ask or a security badge? who ranks blood dust? who converts the beaver? who *doesn't*?

Roy VAN Miki

you propose interface as to-of-on-for-in. kin to entrails. kind to the glob paper weight.

(who said

    "initiated in 1971 and enshrined in the Act

like you; certainly not like you

but: dress codes change, dresses change, the caress of a squished CD indents

. there – surrender pro-nunciates or the cat won't ever escape the bag / lag / lack

. and everyone is smiling

. and no doubt about

saving face takes a toll on the other parts, takes time, takes pillow-talk from ring bearers

                                    so, which codex doesn't
                                  mistake the frog for Basho?

apparently tongues trip over consonants, slam-glide into end-
stop vowels

glottal or otherwise, the explosives clench. then release.
then clench.   then real.

        unpolished; un"ed"ed; a cycle towards music

face it: the shutter speed registers at eleven
                                                  plastic film
                             gauzes the turquoise tête jeune

zip, zap, zooooooom – drop those prairie apples

eight for three
smitten and bitten

                then east.

if i were in a cooley poem

here's the story:

        me and cooley and budde in a car, eh? driving out to
some godforsaken place not one of us can remember
            where   and there were
                        fiction-makers involved

in this kinda story there are always prose writers hovering,
circling, devouring

goddamnit wriggling their way into
        every poetic detail   trying to impose plot
trying to steal the story out from underneath us poets

                                the car
was heading somewhere definite
i remember that   cooley   if pressed
would probably admit to that   and we drove thru the night

that's important to the story have i mentioned
that the car was driving thru the night?

some sort of cooley-slip   then   just the same when
        there haven't been any atrocious puns yet   lets
        you know something's wrong   eh?
something's   not quite on the ballpoint

ah   there we go

the thing is   we were driving
     one of us or all three
who can remember this far from the details?   but
     we all saw it

that's the story: three poets standing

cooley and budde took notes, even drew the image onto a
  wordless page
true to his words: cooley waxed his upper lip, had jack to say
  for himself
budde waned his forehead crease, groaned out two books on
  the spot

we three saw   a blazing hole in the ground
               a wheel a turning

               a meteorite burned deep into snow, the fire
               feeding only on itself

what can I say   we stopped the car

tumbled out and over   the fiery light too perishable to touch
    so we sang
      the cooleyness of its being there

to hell with those other writers   cooley declared bravely
those poor souls who can't believe
in planet matter other
than their own

       sure nuf   when budde flashed his notepad
      they wouldn't read it

man   we shoulda saved our breaths

                        gardeners and prose
                        writers have no
                        imagination when it
                        comes to landscape

hearing the echo of what they'd say, how they'd dismiss our
   prairie miracle
    we piled back in the car   resumed driving, resumed
                                    our searching
toward some bright destination beyond our eyelids
   and when we got there   we told those prose writers
                                   that the sky
pulled a chicken-little, a piece of it plunged – *targetus*
                       interruptus – inside our
                       destination
   and – following the plotline – they didn't believe us

                     so the story ends there

i wish i had more but   the story ends there

(who says a postmodernist can't cater to closure?

embarrassed us they did   those prose writers poured
ridicule and laughter down our exposed necks
insisted that rocks can't burn   especially in the prairie snow

that's a prose writer for you
like snow would make some sorta clinical difference

cooley buffed a pair of new imprints, alleged a sunfall rerelease
budde expanded his geographical repertoire

cowed by all that shame   we huddled in poet-formation
cooley budde and i   we behaved
                        as no self-respecting poet ever shld

we shut up

i don't regret telling them   oh no
poets always have to go around trying to imagine the world
for everyone else   nope
          what i can't forgive myself for is that not one of us
not me   nor budde   nor cooley
                                even once tried
to imagine that that burning creation might
                have been something else entirely

    might have been an electrical storm   say
        or a winged lion

    might have been   a roasting cloud
                            a stone blessing
                                        a displaced waterfall

    might have been   a straw angel   on fire in the
                                                manitoba snow

(Fred stammers, mouth-liquiding)

you wrote "smimming," then couldn't decipher whose handwriting
borrow the letter and you'll have to return it before the end of day
the snake's wet, you shouldn't tear Asia's elephant, not even when it dips into Nelson
this is a *tres pas*-de-dying dance; I wouldn't want Loki passing on the body
a groin pact, or a tongue freeze, welcome to hunger
more artifakes belong in this poem than any other current
between Caesarian harvests, you plan for fragmented grammar
by whom?
tell me the shed doesn't sit pretty
you're pretty mad
but from the mouth, it looks regular as ice
a crutch may not let you unpractice as much as you detour morning breaks
its fiction is failing to castle the winery, marking days, raining answers onto hinged rules
belong or surprise me
long: a constant fetch

Marlatt days press inside skinflakes

your astronomy gauge, a galaxy formula that calculates at a
    dawdle
caught me, graphic

where else to take the Big Dipper, wheeling, wheeling up
    there in the starshine? a chance tremor and his bosom
    gives birth to a moose – "not the whole story" – but
    who wants the other half?

scribbling thaw-lines and a scarce off-the-record ghosted
    rhyme

        your waving wrists, your tongue an engine in
reverse, your sea belly leaps at the lee, chances the chant . .

        endstop , ,
    a bite more than a planet-ring periphery, amber
    plankton at Vesuvius' non sequitur

                who calls?

) and who remedies

"paws to eyes" – the galaxy still pouring, the blood trickles on

Jeune tulip buds with a nosebleed; half a solar system roams your eyelids

; ; inside your ferocious stone hugs

belated Eriń Mour. postcard

When you say, "English is hypothetical," I sneeze loudly, and pontificate on the history of breath. You are not amoozed. "As long as the insides stay *in*," you nap. What's uppity about 47 fathers defending lopsided moustaches? The doctrine or the principle? A business card replicates a poem. Translated. Kissed. Don't wait until Galicia moves. It's just a morsel of Theatre, a frame of falling.

Webb Ghastlies and Anti-Ghastlies

Dear Phylly: What follows is a sort of rant, a champagne-laden, bowl-shaped, opal and naked harangue. Alongside you, not hurtling. They say you are solely a woman, and that you write poetry that doesn't mess up the universe. They're wrong: Pauline still reads the books you haven't yet written. She's plotting to reinvent herself as D-eye-anna with an "I" and to change the course of Canadian coffin texts. You refuse to publish because you refuse to write. So they say. How am I to respond? What imitation? What emulation? You write of the "Baby *Ex Machina*" as if we recognize that baby, as if the Machina is never *In*. Someday, your autobiography will explode and I shall become ugly. If lucky. You once said an animal cannot be separated from its animus. Trio. Will you feed yourself forever on them on them on them? Will I? Pumping blood, your Venus fly-trap undercover spider opens a ventricle. A spy spied. By whom? you may ask. By the useful. By the dozen. By the sliver of the zinc-plated satellite. Sometimes I hear you writing in between the inbetweens. Because after condemned flames, what? Charlatans, rogues, the usual muse stand-ins. I won't listen, but Pauline keeps reading with my fingertips.

Not Christakos Hieroglyphs

the first time, I didn't understand the oasis-missing ellipses. I neglected the diesel boat and the broad "Montréal Ache." You promise to wipe. under. the. oval. But I know better now. I know how to read the line over bumps and turns and even New York gutters. Which sweater folds purple? Which woman coerces rock? Your blood blooming. A brood. This is not the timepiece, not the placemat, not the knot in my intestine-shaped stomach. But.

A grey light hovers over the city. Not quite down. A piece of clunk-clunk-clunk falls against the house's carcass, a burnt retinal freeze on the front. Not grenade welfare. You challenge the "convenient character actor," but who pays his wages when he's dismissed from the page? An ongoing fire witness, waiting in the wings. I wrote: fire witches, but you proof my accidents. The sky breaks and breaks and breaks, and my clitoris chimes. Not in chorus.

Picking on telephone wires isn't fair – it's above, but beneath you. The earth tattles, and I refuse the refuse. Hallowe'en pitchforks not the only way to delegate cutlery, but it's the tradition we clutch. Like grass stems. Like glass flutes. Like like. Promise me you'll continue to feed language to tongues. You see savory and you taste itch. Not in trio.

Machines can spit the farthest. Not a contest. stars. crust. urine. Not a list. This has been your huge self. From me, on the day of Goodbye. Your palms, your torso, your split olfactory nerves, "like water, throbbing."

What she places alongside the lips include: stamps, pumpkin rust, a floral bedspread, four swans, and of course her vagina. Exquisite cunt left a long time ago, so we're stuck with the medical. Check the schedule, another eye skeleton vivisection. As you write running, tell me again what crashes out of your mouth?

The Kensington cafés exude porcelain. Chubby, but for the twelve clay goblets. You allege the art of burning, but I view the train, I reach the hill, shield matches from the snow.

Anachronisms love a parachute. Or overhead baggage on the European train. Belgrade or Turkey. Not too far, but close to the border where.

eyelids / in the Dionne Brand streets

now that I inhabit Ontario
your parched city understands me

declare doorways / declare corners / track phrase scars

some undertake sedition by how water
dries opals, lakeside

as if the prosthetic
conversations
you pledge through your cipher mouth

prolong the long   in long
in damp passing lanes   in lidded furrows

rank this moment, this pin on the map
travel up slopes
where we meet on the edge of concrete bellies
skin curled over knuckles and wrists and hips
a bout of home-envy, a thirst speeding against the forehead
begone

how hard is it to find
Waddington words in a worn world
where Miriam's merely a magician

Typewriterfolds:

her tiger lilies ripen into
a comic laurel wreath
when a rabbi
uncoils her
(she didn't levitate
the Hero's timewheel
witchcraft
held paper
cells in the wooden sink
in the apron of April)
Sunday cucumbers
of loosened blushings
dwelling in Milton's fields
a vampire daylight
the frogs forgot
to burp her their
archaic alphabet
slogans,

      she swallowed drowns;
she swallowed paperweight languages
sounding round her words
falling love showers,

she foresaw sunfingers
Chinese kites
in her bones
  and under her knuckles
the asphalt converted
  to crabgrass
strewn with threeleaf
armadillos and porcupines
cathedral papyrus
  here and here
with blue sailors.

  she unshuffled
parrot rhymes she stopped
for words she leaned
she inked the earth beating
under her feet she hisshissed
anti-municipalities to break tarded
their miniature golf
abuzzing and abending
she designed the see-saw
ghosting and powdering
their floating sourgrass
she proofed
  the Second Coming as a Merry-Go-Round.

And she captured
  THEN
dusted those shoulds

papier-machéd rhymes in Manitoba !
she tilted
       for the rhymes
she fossilized
       for the verbs;
monkey bars   and the metronome
in the floating sourgrass
alphabets skyhangs   and her
       in the crabgrass
ferrying
       for leaf-language
fossilizing for rhymes.

Who am I nuzzling
for strawberries in January
an opal me?
No nightskating for me   here
will never rescue orphan rhymes
here will never paint
       brass words
Does anticipating the fourthcorner sway back
Jamaican prairie

the verbal salt
       playing atop porcupines
strewn with swarth
stressing accents?
Until insect-legged
Human Theys circulate

art fluent and yes-ed
miles over years underlined and
plunging among you
thousandfolded
in a shimmering threeleaf
etcetera

Acknowledgements

I wish to thank the following for ongoing lit dialogues, constant encouragement and boosts, steep criticism and poem-tree love: Pauline Butling, Louis Cabri, Sally Chivers, Debra Dudek, Susan Holbrook, Susan Holloway, John Humphrey, Robert Kroetsch, Melanie Little, Margaret, Roland, & Yvonne Markotić, Suzette Mayr, Laura McLeod, Roy Miki, Rosemary Nixon, Meredith and Peter Quartermain, Nikki Reimer, Jacqueline Turner, and Fred Wah.

A good chunk of "Widows & Orphans" appeared as a Nomados chapbook by the same name, published in Vancouver by Meredith and Peter Quartermain. Ryan Fitzpatrick published "Big Vocabulary" in a Calgary chapbook, also by that name. "The mask off, but the mitts on," "succular," and "seven slurpees for," appeared in *Rampike* magazine, published by Karl Jirgens. "Sunday Morning, Making a Break" appeared in a special issue of *The Capilano Review*, edited by Jenny Penberthy. "Van in AV" appeared in a special issue of *West Coast Line*, edited by Michael Barnholden and Fred Wah. rob mclennan published "Jan 9" as an above/ground broadside. "Letter from Joyville," appeared in the Coach House anthology, *71 (+) Poems for GB*, edited by Jean Baird, David McFadden, and George Stanley. The *Windsor Review* published seven early versions of poems from the "Widows & Orphans" section, edited by Susan Holbrook and Marty Gervais; *filling Station*, edited by Natalie Simpson and the *fS* collective, published two from this section; *The Capilano Review*, edited by Ryan Knighton, published eight earlier versions; *In Grave Ink,* edited by Lindsay Tipping, published four; two appeared in *Bemused,* edited by Jocelyn Grosse; the Kootenay School of Writing collective magazine, *W,* published two; two poems appeared in *Contemporary Verse 2,* edited by the collective; four poems appeared in *West Coast Line,* edited by Colin Browne, Miriam Nichols, and Jerry Zaslove; and five others exist in *Post-Prairie,* edited by Jon Paul Fiorentino and Robert Kroetsch.

Cheers and thank you to Don Denton, for kind permission to use his terrific photo.

Excessive thanks to Kate Hargraves for an incredible cover, Sarah Mitchell for permission to use the image from one of her exquisite handmade books, and Jay MillAr for the entire fabulous book design.

An over-the-top, grandiose, extravagant thanks to Hazel Millar and Jay MillAr, and the entire BookThug publishing team: splendid!

An extra especially-special thank-you to those who read all or part (or repeated parts) of this manuscript and gave me specific and wildly appreciated feedback: Louis Cabri, Suzette Mayr, Rosemary Nixon – best editors ever.

NICOLE MARKOTIĆ is a fiction writer and poet who has published two novels (*Yellow Pages,* a prose narrative of Alexander Graham Bell and *Scrapbook of My Years as a Zealot,* which takes on notions of friendship, adult relationships with one's mother, the holocaust, and disability), two previous books of poetry (*Connect the Dots* and *Minotaurs & Other Alphabets*), and the chapbook, *more excess,* which won the bpNichol Chapbook award. A former resident of Calgary, she now teaches English Literature and Creative Writing at the University of Windsor, specializing in Canadian Literature, Poetry, Children's Literature, and Disability Studies. She has edited a collection of poetry by Dennis Cooley, *By Word of Mouth,* has worked as a freelance editor, has edited special issues for the literary journals *Open Letter* and *Tessera,* and has co-edited a collection of critical essays on film and disability. She was poetry editor for Red Deer Press for six years and has recently joined the NeWest literary board as one of its fiction editors. She publishes a poetry chapbook series, Wrinkle Press, which includes work by Robert Kroetsch, Nikki Reimer, and Fred Wah.

Colophon

Manufactured as the First Edition of
Bent at the Spine in the spring of 2012
by BookThug. Distrinuted in Canada by
The Literary Press Group www.lpg.ca.
Distributed in the United States by Small
Press Distribution www.spdbooks.org.
Shop online at www.bookthug.ca

Front cover concept by Kate Hargreaves
Type + design by Jay MillAr